TRINITY GUILDHALL

Electronic Keyboard Grade 5

Pieces & Technical Work
for Trinity Guildhall examinations

2011-2013

Published by
Trinity College London
Registered office:
89 Albert Embankment
London SE1 7TP UK

T +44 (0)20 7820 6100
F +44 (0)20 7820 6161
E music@trinityguildhall.co.uk
www.trinityguildhall.co.uk

Registered in the UK
Company no. 02683033
Charity no. 1014792

Copyright © 2010 Trinity College London

Second impression, April 2011

Unauthorised photocopying is illegal.
No part of this publication may be copied or reproduced in any
form or by any means without the prior permission of the publisher.

Printed in England by Halstan & Co. Ltd, Amersham, Bucks.

PLEASE SET UP FOR THE NEXT PIECE

* This C♯ can be played in the RH (for one bar) if the stretch is not comfortable.

PLEASE SET UP FOR THE NEXT PIECE

GROUP A

Danse macabre

Camille Saint-Saëns
arr. Joanna Clarke

Voices: Strings (dual voice Xylophone)/Violin (dual voice Strings)
Style: Waltz (Viennese)

GROUP A

Three Little Maids from School

from *The Mikado*

Gilbert and Sullivan
arr. Nancy Litten

Voices: Marimba (dual voice Piano)/Choir (dual voice Strings)
Style: Polka

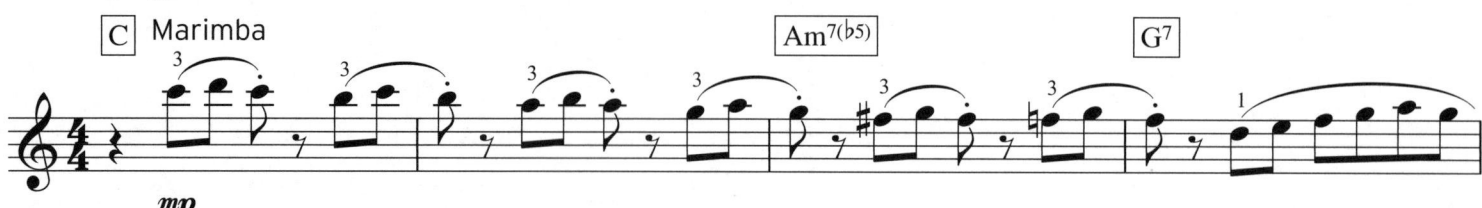
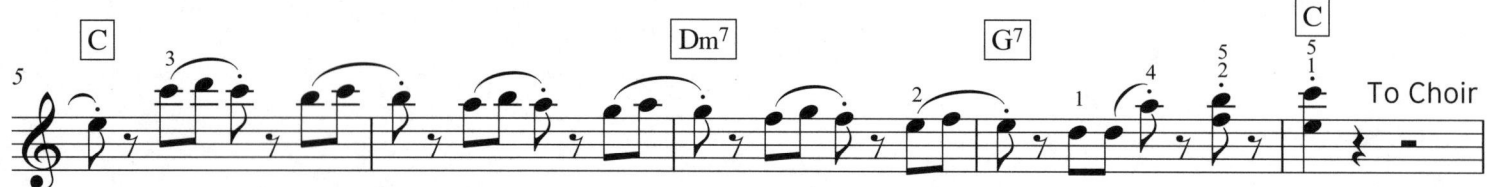
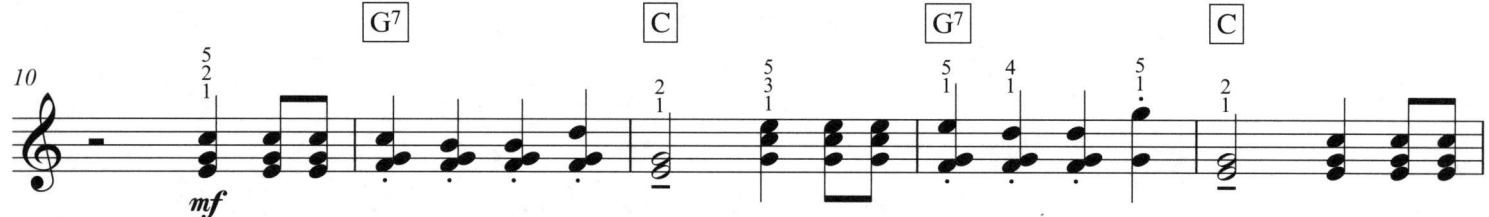
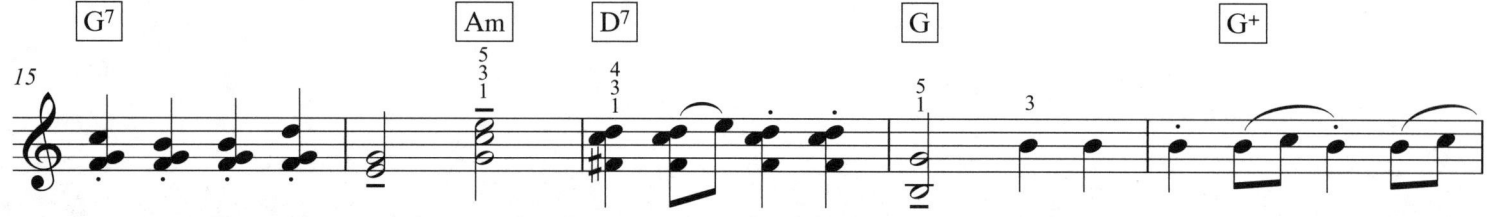

This piece is published under licence from Nancy Litten.

GROUP B

Improvisation

Montuno

Paul Burnell

GROUP B

Birthday Bash

Nancy Litten

Voices: Brass/Alto Saxophone (dual voice Sax. Ensemble)
Style: Big Band

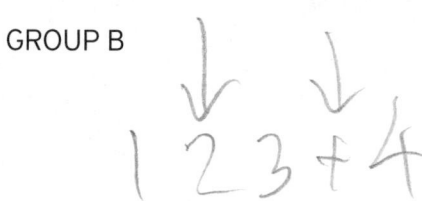

GROUP B

Bollywood Love Song

Kuljit Bhamra

* Applicable from bar 7 onwards.

This piece is published under licence from Kuljit Bhamra.

PLEASE SET UP FOR THE NEXT PIECE

Technical Work

All sections i) to iii) to be prepared. Sections i) and ii) must be performed from memory; the music may be used for Section iii).

i) Scales

The following scales to be performed in piano voice with auto-accompaniment off, hands together (unless otherwise stated), ♩ = 110, *legato* and **mf**:

Db and B major (two octaves)
Bb and G# minor (two octaves): candidate's choice of *either* harmonic *or* melodic *or* natural minor
G harmonic minor contrary motion scale (two octaves)
Chromatic scale in similar motion starting on Db and B (two octaves)
Blues scale starting on F and A, right hand only, straight and swing rhythm (two octaves)

Db major scale (two octaves)

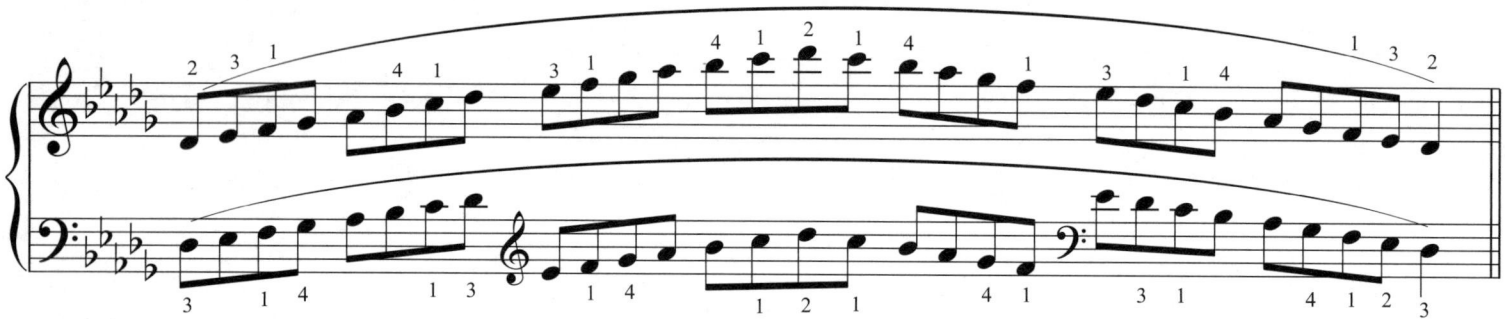

B major scale (two octaves)

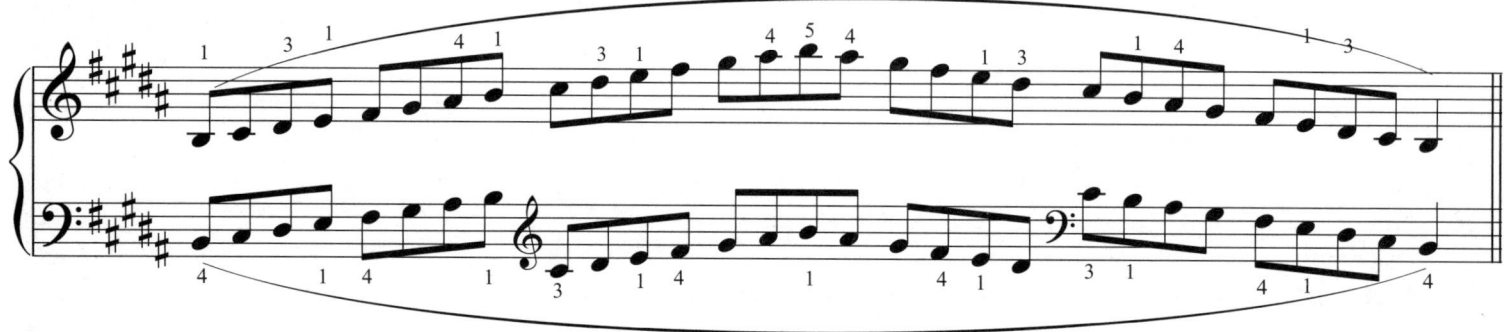

Bb minor scale: harmonic (two octaves)

B♭ minor scale: melodic (two octaves)

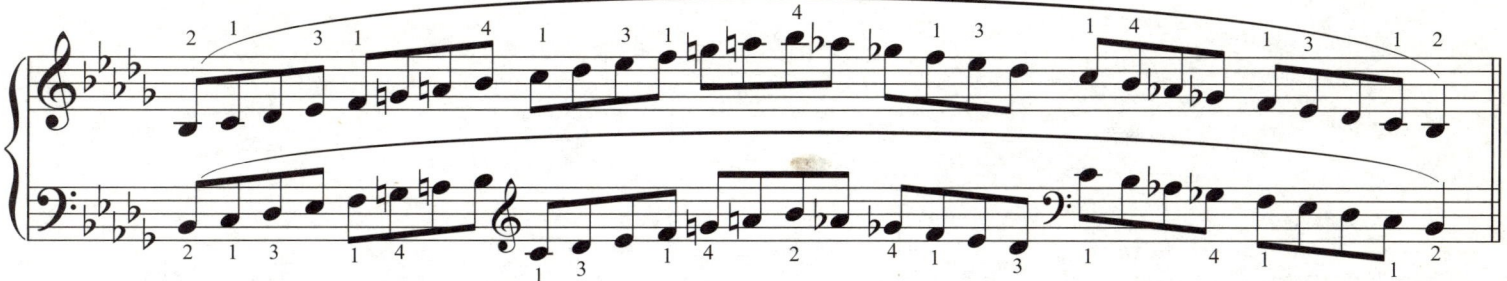

B♭ minor scale: natural (two octaves)

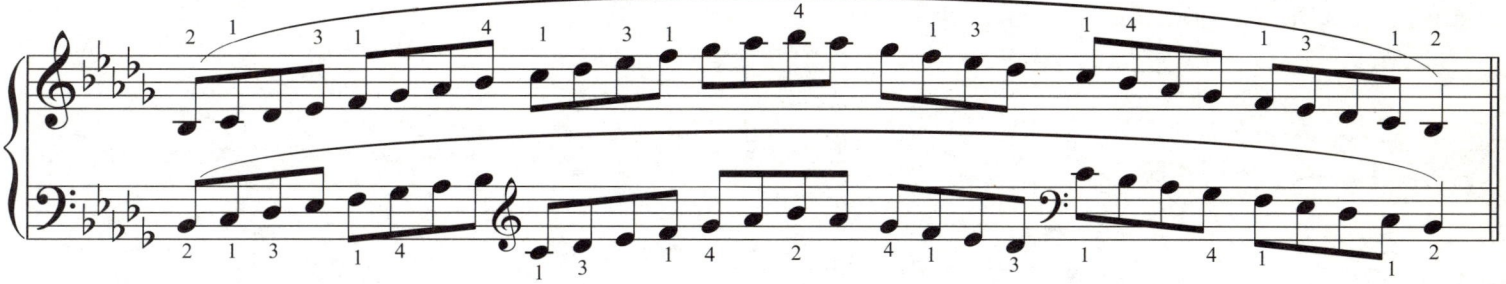

G♯ minor scale: harmonic (two octaves)

G♯ minor scale: melodic (two octaves)

G♯ minor scale: natural (two octaves)

G harmonic minor contrary motion scale (two octaves)

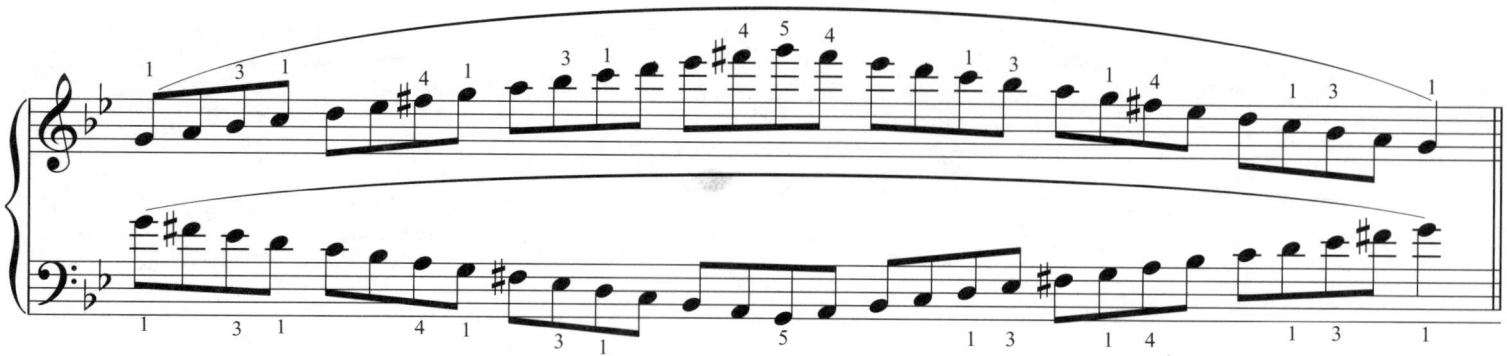

Chromatic scale in similar motion starting on D♭ (two octaves)

Chromatic scale in similar motion starting on B (two octaves)

Blues scale starting on F (two octaves)

Right hand

Blues scale starting on A (two octaves)

Right hand

ii) Chord knowledge

The following to be performed with the bass note in the left hand and three notes of the chord in the right hand, in piano voice with auto-accompaniment off:

Chords of D♭^{maj7}, B^{maj7}, B♭m^7, G♯m^7, B♭m^{maj7}, G♯m^{maj7}, D♭^{6}, B^6, B♭m^6, G♯m^6

Perfect cadence in C, G and F major

please turn over

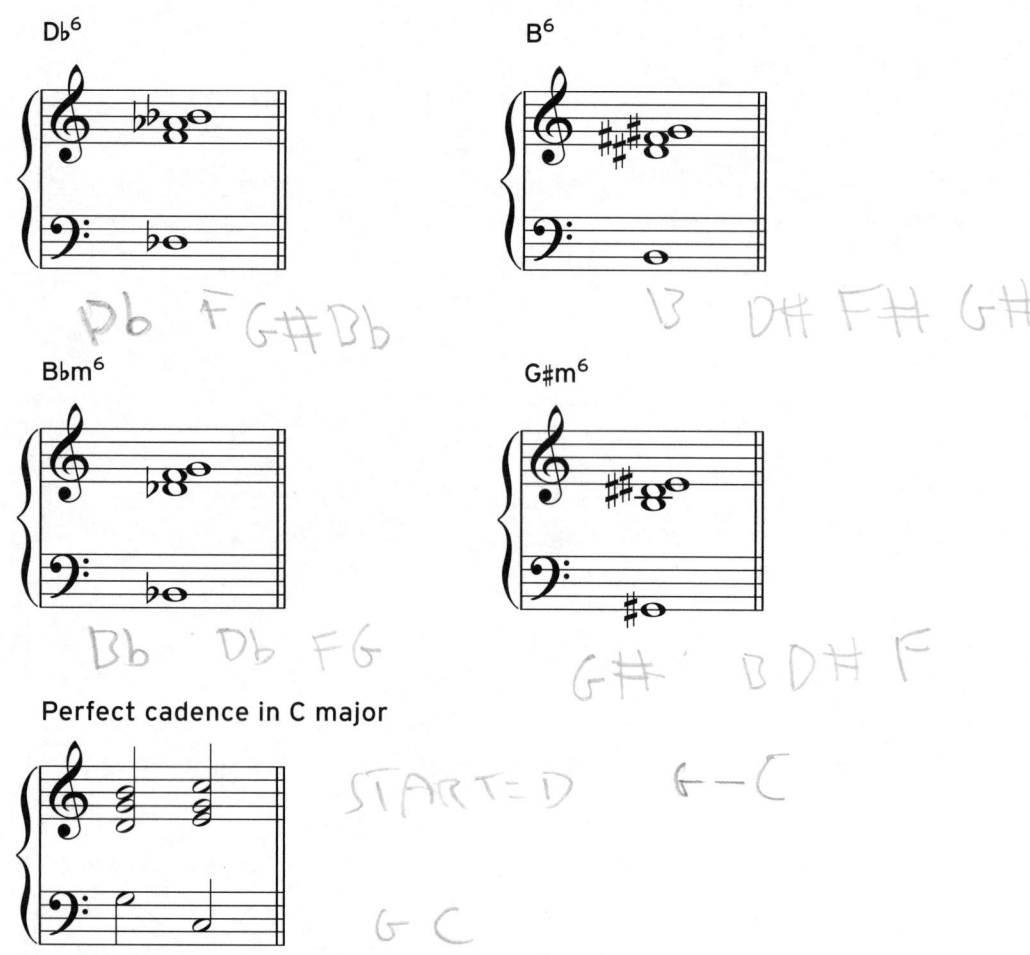

Db F G# Bb

B D# F# G#

Bb Db F G

G# B D# F

Perfect cadence in C major

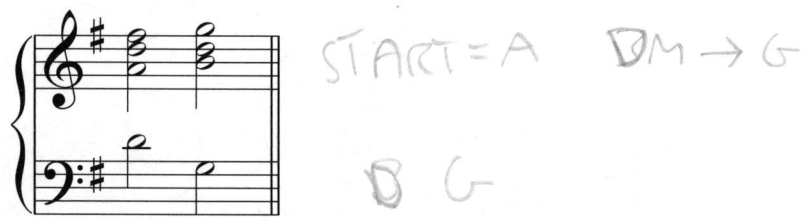

START=D F—C

G C

Perfect cadence in G major

START=A DM→G

D G

Perfect cadence in F major

START=G C→F

C F

iii) Exercises

Candidate to prepare all three exercises.

1. Late Night Blues – bass clef reading and finger dexterity
Voice: Piano
Style: Swing

2. Master Blues – arpeggios and chord use [fingered chords must be used]
Voice: Jazz Organ
Style: Jazz Funk/Soul/Blues

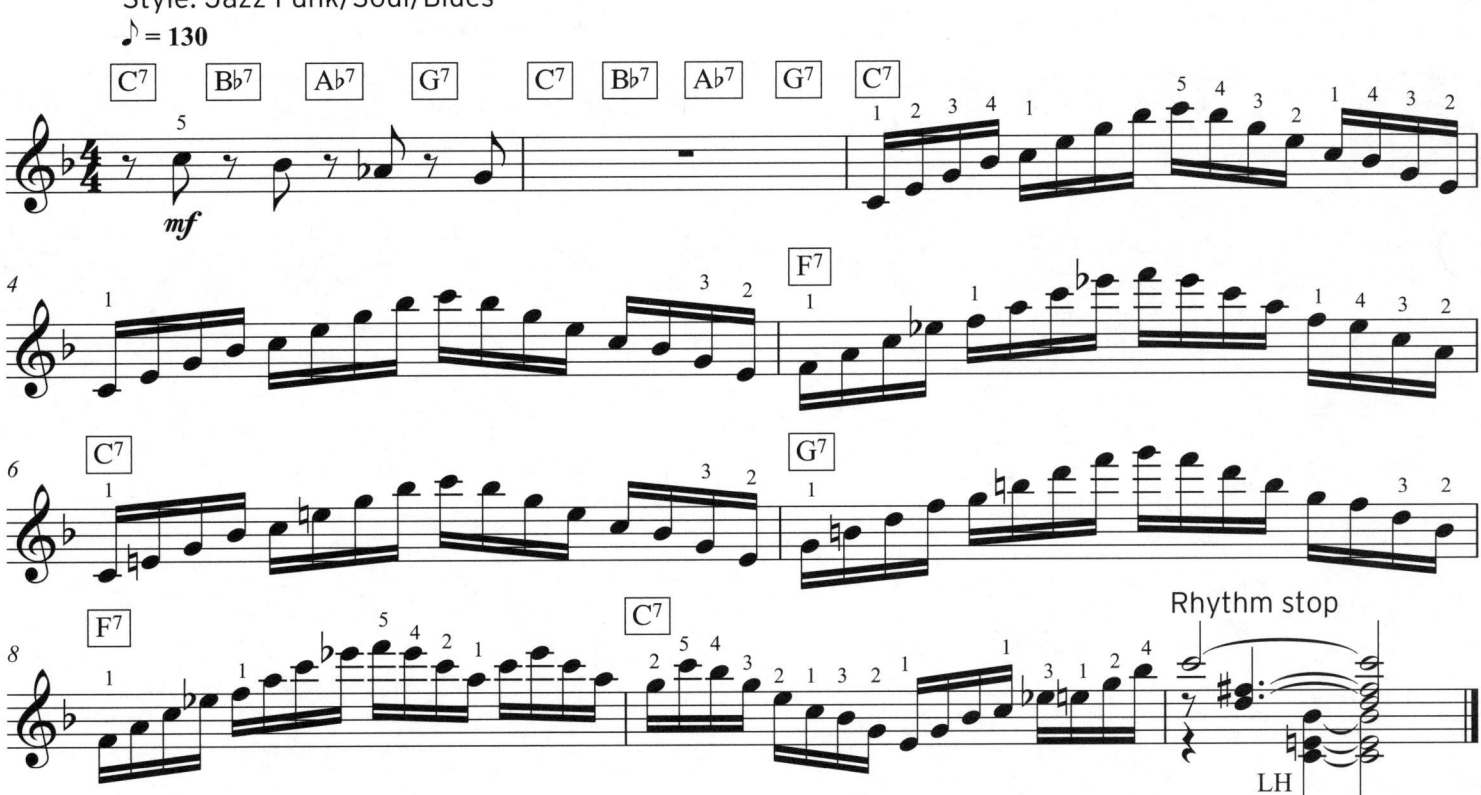

3. Swingin' It – using keyboard functions